LOOK WHAT FEET CAN DO

LOOK What ANIMALS Can Do

LOOK WHAT FEET CAN DO

BY D. M. SOUZA

LOOK What ANIMALS Can Do

Lerner Publications Company · Minneapolis

photo on page 2: **Verreaux's sifaka, a kind of lemur that lives in Madagascar, appears to dance on its hind feet. Actually, this is how these lemurs walk.**

Lerner Publications Company
A division of Lerner Publishing Group
241 First Avenue North
Minneapolis, MN 55401 U.S.A.

Website address: www.lernerbooks.com

Library of Congress Cataloging-in-Publication Data

Souza, D. M. (Dorothy M.)
  Look what feet can do / by D. M. Souza.
    p.   cm. — (Look what animals can do)
  Includes bibliographical references and index.
  ISBN-13: 978–0–7613–9460–0 (lib. bdg. : alk. paper)
  ISBN-10: 0–7613–9460–5 (lib. bdg. : alk. paper)
    1. Foot—Juvenile literature. I. Title. II. Series; Souza, D. M. (Dorothy M.) Look what animals can do.
  QL950.7.S68 2007
  573.9'98—dc22   2005032478

Manufactured in the United States of America
1 2 3 4 5 6 – DP – 12 11 10 09 08 07

TABLE OF CONTENTS

LOOK AROUND   7

DIGGING MACHINE   10

DEADLY FEET   14

STICKY HAIRS   18

WATER SKIS   22

COZY FEET   26

FISHING FEET   30

ONE SLIMY FOOT   34

A PARADE OF FEET   38

GLOSSARY   44

FURTHER READING   45

INDEX   47

LOOK AROUND.
FEET ARE EVERYWHERE.

Feet are walking, running, skipping, dancing, kicking, and climbing. Acrobats are hanging upside down by their feet. Children with wheels on their feet are skating. Adults with skis on their feet are sailing down hillsides. It's awesome what human feet can do.

Feet come in all colors and sizes. They help people move from one place to another.

Other animals do amazing things with their feet too. An ostrich, for example, is the world's largest living bird. Its feet are powerful. One kick from an ostrich's foot can kill a lion.

Some animals use their feet to catch fish. Some climb glass walls or walk on water. Other animals flirt, send messages, or fight with their feet. We're about to meet a few of these far-out feet.

These ostriches are running. The claw at the end of their front toe helps them grip the ground.

DIGGING MACHINE

The meadow is still and quiet. A badger catches the scent of a gopher. The badger flops on its stomach and puts its chin on the edge of the gopher's hideout.

Next, the badger's huge front feet scoop up dirt and toss it under its belly. Its back feet kick everything into the air. The animal looks as if it's swimming in clouds of dirt and dust. In minutes the badger will enjoy a meal. Few **prey** can escape once this animal starts digging.

When digging, badgers loosen the dirt with their front feet and push it under their belly. Then they kick it out of the hole with their back feet.

The badger sometimes travels as many as 8 miles (13 kilometers) in one night. When the animal gets tired, it stops. Its feet dig a **burrow** where the badger can nap. If a bear or mountain lion corners it, those same feet work at top speed. They can dig an escape hole in less than two minutes.

Claws on the badger's front feet are almost as long as its toes. Skin between the toes gives them added strength. Hind feet are spoon-shaped to scoop away dirt. Everything about the badger makes it a perfect digging machine.

A badger's front feet each have five toes with claws up to 2 inches (5 cm) long.

DEADLY FEET

A red-tailed hawk looks down from a perch high in a tree. Its scaly, knobby feet rest on a branch. Four toes are tipped with long, pointed nails. The bird's nails are called **talons**. They are as sharp as daggers.

The hawk spots a snake moving in the field below. Jumping into the wind with outstretched wings, the bird flies up. It circles the field a few times and then dives.

A red-tailed hawk sits very still high up in a tree, waiting to spot its prey. The eyesight of a hawk is eight times as powerful as a human's.

Just before reaching the snake, the hawk
stretches out its legs and toes. Feet lock onto the prey.
Talons pierce its flesh until the snake is lifeless. In
minutes the hawk flies away with its meal.

The red-tailed hawk is not the only bird with
deadly feet. Other hawks, falcons, vultures, eagles,
and owls have them too. These birds are known as
raptors. Long ago the word meant "to grab by force."
And that's what raptors do with their feet.

When getting ready to attack its prey, the hawk
stiffens its legs and pushes its talons forward. It
uses its tail and wings to slow down.

STICKY HAIRS

A gecko climbs a glass wall and walks across a ceiling. Then it hangs in place by only one toe. How does it do that?

Beneath each of the gecko's toes are thousands of thin hairs. They are ten times thinner than a single hair on your head. A million gecko hairs could easily fit on the top of a penny.

Gecko hairs may be thin, but they are strong. A single one could hold an ant. Several thousand can easily hold the gecko as it hangs by one toe.

A gecko can walk up glass and across ceilings because of its amazing feet.

When the gecko takes a step, its hairs roll onto the surface until they stick. As the animal moves along, it peels the hairs away like tape. Stick, peel, stick, peel. The gecko never slips or falls.

Scientists are trying to make hairs like those on the gecko's feet. They hope someday to attach them to material humans can wear. Then maybe we will be able to walk up glass walls and across ceilings like the gecko. Stick, peel, stick, peel.

The undersides of a gecko's feet have sole and toe pads. These pads are covered with around 500,000 sticky hairs.

WATER SKIS

A lizard suns itself next to a stream in Central America. The creature belongs to a group of lizards in the iguana family known as **basilisks**. Like dinosaurs, basilisks can run on two feet.

The lizard's large, bulging eyes look nervously around. The creature senses that something is coming. It may be time to run.

A snake crawls into the open. Quickly the lizard stands up on its hind legs. Its large, webbed feet race over the ground. Sharp claws barely touch the earth.

Basilisks have long legs and long toes with sharp claws. This helps them run fast.

The lizard reaches the stream's edge, but it does not stop. It runs across the water and does not sink. The lizard's feet are so big it's as though it's wearing water skis.

The basilisk can run about 7 miles (11 km) an hour. As long as it moves quickly, it will not sink in the water. If it slows down, it will go under.

Even if the lizard sinks, it still has a chance to escape. Its webbed feet help it swim below the surface. **Predators** look around, but they cannot find the water-skiing lizard. Now you see it; now you don't.

This lizard is running fast across the water. If it slows down, it will drop into the water and swim the rest of the way.

COZY FEET

In March, cold winter winds blow across Antarctica. The sun never shines, and the seas are ice. It is so cold that human skin can freeze in seconds.

During this time of year, most animals leave Antarctica for warmer places. But thousands of emperor penguins arrive to find mates. They are the only birds to **breed**, or have their young, during winter.

After a penguin pair mates, the female lays a single egg. The male wriggles the egg onto his feet. Then he covers it with a warm layer of his belly skin.

A male emperor penguin looks at the egg he is keeping warm on his feet.

A few days later, the female penguins leave. They will spend almost two months at sea searching for food. In the meantime, their mates will keep the eggs warm.

Males do nothing but huddle together. They eat nothing and can lose almost half their weight. But the eggs remain warm and safe on their feet.

After the young hatch, the females return and cough up food for their young. Chicks move onto their mothers' feet, and hungry males leave on their own fishing trips. For two more months, the chicks remain cozy and warm on their mothers' feet.

A chick is keeping warm on its mother's feet. When it becomes older, it will wander out on its own.

FISHING FEET

The large pond is dark and still. Suddenly, tiny splashing sounds break the silence. The noises are repeated again and again. Fishing bats are at work.

These unusual bats live near water in Central and South America. They have long hind legs and feet much bigger than those of other bats. Their wings are huge.

During the day, the bats sleep in caves, hollow trees, or rock piles. A few even rest under large, empty turtle shells. All their hideouts smell fishy.

Fishing bats have long hind legs and huge hind feet. Their feet are two to four times longer than those of other bats.

When it's time to eat, the bats fly out, zigzagging close to the water. They listen for small fish feeding just below the surface. All at once, they hit the water with their feet. Then they sweep the surface with long, sharp claws.

Bats that catch a fish in their claws may eat it while they fly. Some may take it to a perch. Others store their treat in special cheek pouches and continue fishing.

Before dawn the bats return to their hideouts. Many sleep together in the same place. There they rest until it's time to go fishing again.

Fishing bats sweep for fish by dragging their long claws about an inch beneath the surface of the water.

ONE SLIMY FOOT

The sun has disappeared. A slug moves out of its hiding place under a rock. On top of its head are two long, fleshy horns. Each horn has an eye on its tip. Beneath the long horns are two shorter ones with two more eyes.

The slug moves slowly. From one end of its body to the other, muscles rise and fall like tiny waves. These muscles are part of the slug's one and only foot. They are its pedal power. They help it surf over the ground.

Slugs are related to snails, clams, oysters, and scallops. All have only one foot.

As the slug moves, slime oozes from its body. Slime acts as a carpet for the slug's big foot. Instead of footprints, the animal leaves behind a trail of slime.

The slug climbs a wall, but does not slip. It surfs over broken glass and pieces of sharp metal. But nothing cuts or scratches its body. Slime protects it.

When the sun appears again in the sky, the slug turns around. It picks up the scent of its trail and follows it back to its hideout. Slowly it moves along on its big, slimy foot.

The slug leaves behind a trail of slime that protects its body as it travels.

A PARADE OF FEET

Many animals use their feet as tools. For example, mole crickets can turn their front feet into shovels. Beavers comb their fur with their front claws and hind feet. Otters catch food with their front feet.

A sea otter holds its meal with its front feet while eating.

Did you know that houseflies taste with their feet? They have hundreds of tiny hairs on the bottom of their feet. As the insect walks, these hairs signal when it reaches food. You may have seen flies rubbing their legs and feet together. They try to keep them clean and ready. At any moment they may walk across a treat.

Houseflies are always rubbing their feet together to keep them clean for their next meal.

Butterflies also taste with their feet. When they land on a drop of syrup, their tongues roll out like party favors. Butterflies sense when their feet have found something sweet to drink.

Butterflies roll out their long tongues to sip nectar from flowers.

Blue-footed boobies are birds that live on the Galápagos Islands of Ecuador. They have bright blue feet. During mating season, males wave their feet to catch the attention of females.

The male blue-footed booby is waving his feet to catch the attention of the female. This is called courting.

Some animals, such as deer, horses, elk, and roosters, fight with their feet. A kangaroo's feet pack a double punch. While the animal boxes with its front feet, its hind feet can deliver a knockout blow.

Kangaroos are well known for their powerful boxing abilities.

Scientists believe that elephants signal one another by stomping their feet. Elephants as far away as 20 miles (32 km) are able to pick up the message. They do it through their feet. Now those are far-out feet!

Elephants can feel vibrations from the ground in their feet. This helps them receive messages from other elephants.

GLOSSARY

basilisks: lizards that can run on their hind legs

breed: to produce offspring

burrow: a hole or tunnel in the ground

claws: nails on the feet of some animals

predators: an animal that hunts other animals

prey: an animal that is hunted and killed by another animal

raptors: birds of prey, such as hawks, falcons, or eagles

talons: nails on the feet of birds of prey

FURTHER READING

BOOKS

Hess, Nina, and John Kanzler. *Whose Feet?* London: Random House Books for Young Readers, 2004.

Lock, Deborah. *Feathers, Flippers, & Feet.* New York: Dorling Kindersley Publishing, 2004.

Miles, Elizabeth. *Legs and Feet.* Chicago: Heinemann Library, 2002.

Schwartz, David. *Animal Feet.* Milwaukee: Gareth Stevens Publishing, 2000.

Whittaker, Nicola. *Feet.* Milwaukee: Gareth Stevens Publishing, 2002.

WEBSITES

Badgers

http://www.badgers.org/when.html#c7

This website has badger facts and photos.

Fishing Bats

http://www.photovault.com/Link/Animals/Mammals/Bats/
Species/FishingBat.html

This website contains photos of a fishing bat making a catch.

Red-Tailed Hawks

http://www.yahooligans.yahoo.com/content/animals/species/
2389.html

Learn more about red-tailed hawks on this site.

INDEX

Page numbers in *italics* refer to illustrations.

acrobats, 7

Antarctica, 26

badger, 10–13

basilisk, 22, 25. *see also* lizard

bats, 30–33

beavers, 38

blue-footed boobies, 41

butterflies, 40

Central America, 22, 30

claws: of badger, 13; of bats, 33; of beavers, 38; of lizards, 22

deer, 42

eagles, 16

egg, of emperor penguin, 26–28, *27*

elephants, 43

elk, 42

emperor penguins, 26–29

falcons, 16

feet: of badger, 10, 13; of bats, 30, 33; of beavers, 38; of blue-footed boobies, 41; of butterflies, 40; of elephants, 43; of emperor penguins, 26, 28; of gecko, 18, *20*, 21; of houseflies, 39; of humans, 7; of kangaroo, 42; of lizards, 22, 25; of mole crickets, 38; of ostriches, 8; of

otters, 38; of red-tailed hawk, 14, 16; of slugs, 34, 37; webbed, 25

gecko, 18–21

gopher, 10

horses, 42

houseflies, 39

kangaroo, 42

lizard, 22–25

mole crickets, 38

ostrich, 8, 9

otters, 38

owls, 16

predators, 25

prey, 10, 14, 16

raptors, 16

red-tailed hawk, 14–17

roosters, 42

slime, *36*, 37

slug, 34–37

talons, 14, *15*, 16, *17*

toes: of badger, 13; of gecko, 18, *20*; of red-tailed hawk, 14, 16

Verreaux's sifaka, 2, 4

vultures, 16

PHOTO ACKNOWLEDGMENTS

Images reproduced with permission from:
© Harvey Martin/Peter Arnold, Inc., p. 2; © argus/Peter Arnold, Inc., p. 6; © OSF/Peter Lillie/Animals Animals, p. 8; © Stephen J. Krasemann/Photo Researchers, Inc., p. 11; © Jeanne White/Photo Researchers, Inc., p. 12; © M. H. Sharp/Photo Researchers, Inc., p. 15; © Anthony Mercieca/Photo Researchers, Inc., p. 17; © James Robinson/Animals Animals, p. 19; © Zigmund Leszcynski/Animals Animals, pp. 20, 23; © Joe McDonald/Visuals Unlimited, p. 24; © Bruno P. Zehnder/Peter Arnold, Inc., p. 27; © Art Wolfe/Photo Researchers, Inc., p. 29; © Frans Lanting/CORBIS, p. 31; © Stephen Dalton/Animals Animals, p. 32; © Jim Zipp/Photo Researchers, Inc., p. 35; © Rick Poley/Visuals Unlimited, p. 36; © Pat & Tom Leeson/Photo Researchers, Inc., p. 38; © Raymond Mendez/Animals Animals, p. 39; © BIOS/Peter Arnold Inc., p. 40; © John and Barbara Gerlach/Visuals Unlimited, p. 41; © Gunter Ziesler/Peter Arnold, Inc., p. 42; © Francois Savigny/Animals Animals, p. 43.

Front cover: © Wolfgang Kaehler/CORBIS.